GOING WILD!

Written by Jillian Powell
Illustrated by Mel Sharp

Mum, Dad and I went to a wild animal park. We drove through the big open gates.

Below a map, it said:
Don't open car windows!
Don't feed the animals!

I could see a herd of deer roaming freely.

They were sipping from a wide river.

"Slow down, Dad," I said.
"Did you hear that bellow?
Look! Hippos!"

This hippo was swimming in the river. I took a quick snap.

A buffalo came to take a gulp from the river.
"He is **so** big!" I said.

A keeper drove a trailer of hay through the park.
We followed him to the camels.

The keeper pointed to a tiger in the shadow of a boulder. I could see its golden eyes.

"Don't go too close!" the keeper called.
I took a second snap.

There were baby apes playing in the trees.
They jumped on the car.
They were so bold!

"Hello!" I said.
I got a close-up of a nose!

Some zebras ran away as we approached. Then I froze!

There was a big, lone lion dozing in the sunshine. He had a jumbo-sized bone.

"Time to go home," said Dad. I hope we can go back to the wild animal park soon!